THEN & NOW

MORRO BAY

Opposite: Two icons of Morro Bay begin this look at the past and present of the town. Morro Rock (el Moro or "the sentinel") first drew the attention of Spanish explorer Juan Cabrillo in 1542. The Williams and Riley pier (or embarcadero), built in the 1920s, was a forerunner of today's Embarcadero, a thriving bay-side business district 2 miles long. (Courtesy Morro Bay Historical Society.)

THEN & NOW

MORRO BAY

Roger Castle and Gary Ream
with photographs by Garry Johnson

This project is dedicated to our wives for their patience and understanding.

ON THE COVER: The Heights was the first residential development outside of the town center. It is located on the west shoulder of Black Hill (called Black Mountain by some) with commanding views of the town, the bay, and the rock. A narrow road leads through the golf course to a tiny parking spot above the development. The rolling hillside to the left, once envisioned as residential, became the championship golf course and state park. (Front cover then, courtesy Adel Costa; now, courtesy Roger Castle. Back cover courtesy Juanita Tolle.)

CONTENTS

ACKNOWLEDGMENTS

In any task of this size, the list of those to thank grows long, and the risk of forgetting someone increases. To all who listened to our requests, responded to our many e-mails and phone calls, and provided us with the very real history presented here, thank you. We could not have been successful without the help you provided. This type of history is about choosing what to show. Even if we did not use your photographs and ideas, know that they helped us in our quest to show the best of Morro Bay's past and present.

We would first thank the Historical Society of Morro Bay and the History Center of San Luis Obispo County for the generous use of their archives. The Morro Bay group's archive of material from Jane Bailey and Dorothy Gates was most useful.

The following individuals were particularly supportive of our project, and we thank them for their extra time and effort: Forrest L. Doud for taking the aerial photograph on page 82 for this book; Juanita Tolle, daughter of William "Bill" Roy, for the use of his collection; Wayne Bickford for the use of his brother Glenn's collection; Lynda Roeller for the other aerial photographs that appear in chapter four; and Schani Siong for the computer graphic on page 95.

Additionally Gary Ream and Roger Castle would like to thank Garry Johnson for so capably taking on photographic and computer responsibilities late in this project.

The original photographers of most of these historical pictures are not the current owners, but where they are known, we have tried to identify them. Many of these were professionals or serious amateurs. Some were everyday folks with a Kodak Brownie. All have created bodies of work that have become the foundation of our town's historical record. Unless otherwise noted, modern pictures without credits were taken by Garry Johnson especially for this book.

INTRODUCTION

When we first heard that Arcadia was beginning a new series of regional histories with a "then and now" format, we were most excited. These kinds of parings have always held great fascination for us. In the process of putting together the Images of America book on Morro Bay, we were sometimes tempted to slip in newer pictures. We are happy to have the opportunity to show how much and how little our city has changed over the years.

History in many ways is about memory. Our task in compiling this book is to spark and preserve memories and in so doing help preserve our history. We hope the book will activate your memories of Morro Bay and/or your favorite town. If it calls to mind tidbits and anecdotes of your times here, please share them with us. If it reminds you of your hometown, we hope you will be moved to record it and share it with others.

Roger Castle
Gary Ream
Garry Johnson
c/o The Historical Society of Morro Bay
P.O. Box 921
Morro Bay, CA 93442-0921

For more in-depth history of Morro Bay, please see the following:

Gates, Dorothy and Jane Bailey. *Morro Bay's Yesterday*. Morro Bay, CA: El Morro Publications, 1982.
www.oldmorrobay.com: A magnificent site by Vic Hanson with many pictures and stories.
www.historycenterslo.org: The History Center of San Luis Obispo County site
www.morrobay.org: The Morro Bay Chamber of Commerce site

CHAPTER 1

THE TOWN AND
ITS BEGINNINGS

This is Morro Bay Boulevard and Main Street about 1900. The building on the left is the town's first general store. According to historian Jane Bailey, it was built by William Maston in 1872. At various times, it was also a grocery store and even a post office before being torn down in the 1970s.

In 1894, Mathias Schneider built a competing store across Morro Bay Boulevard. By the 1950s that site was a service station, and today it is home to Heritage Oaks Bank. (Then, courtesy Historical Society of Morro Bay.)

The first floor of this building at Morro Bay Boulevard and Monterey was built in 1927 by George and Lillie Anderson. Lillie Anderson was postmaster, and half of the building became the new post office (see page 27). They added the second story in 1928. The Andersons had several ventures here, including a dry goods store and (according to Vic Hanson) Morro Bay's first telephone exchange. In the 1950s, when the post office moved, they opened a five and dime store. (Then, courtesy Rosemary and Kay Thorne; now, courtesy Thom Ream.)

THE TOWN AND ITS BEGINNINGS

This building at the southwest corner of Morro Bay Boulevard and Main Street began as a hotel in the early 1920s. It soon became the real estate office of Miller and Murphy's Morro Bay Vista Company and housed visiting prospective clients. The hotel's garage had become the dining room. By the end of the decade, the garage had become Matson's Grocery and Johnson's Bakery used part of the hotel. The bottom floor still exists, housing the Pizza Port restaurant. (Then, courtesy Juanita Tolle.)

The only natural part of today's Embarcadero lies just south of Beach Street. A narrow strip of land below the bluff allowed access except during the highest tides. Note the stairs leading up to Silva's Wharf. The building was a saltwater plunge. According to historian Jane Bailey, it was built around 1925 by "Happy" Wilkens and only operated for a few years. (Then, courtesy Juanita Tolle.)

The town's second business district is the waterfront/Embarcadero area. The narrow strip of land by the bay below the bluff was extended and filled in, with most of the work done during World War II. By the 1950s, business had begun to prosper there. One of the best restaurants (and best employers) was Bud Anderson's Galley. It is seen here as it was in 1965 and in its latest incarnation. (Then, courtesy Anderson family.)

The Kline family was typical of many postwar residents. Neil Kline served in the air force during World War II and followed relatives to Morro Bay after the war ended. Like many residents after the Depression and World War II, he worked many jobs, both in and out of the sea. He bought the lot shown below in 1951, and over the next 30 years built a home and raised four children. (Then, courtesy Roy Kline.)

The potential for development of the land north of town was recognized by developers as early as 1920. (See pages 28–32.) However, due to the Depression and legal issues, growth of the residential district did not really begin until the mid-1950s, when this picture was taken. Today the area is home to businesses and motels along the highway and heavily built out with single-family homes. (Then, courtesy Roy Kline.)

When legal issues were finally resolved, this area, known as Morro Del Mar, began building in earnest. Developers, contractors, and local construction workers all benefited, as did the many families who purchased homes. This mini-development, created by future county supervisor Jesse Drake, was a typical project. Some of these homes on Seaview Street still exist. (Then, courtesy Wayne Bickford.)

THE TOWN AND ITS BEGINNINGS

One of the last remnants of the airport to fade away was the Airport Café. It was located directly across the old two-lane highway (now Quintana Road) at the south end of the runway. The building, with its 1950s-style false front, was occasionally a café and often a private residence for many years. It was torn down to make way for a modern commercial building. (Then, courtesy Thom Ream.)

Miller and Murphy, real estate developers in the 1920s, sold view lots on the rolling land on the west facing slope of Black Hill. Today houses and fully grown trees make the view harder to find.

A small parking spot above the golf course was favored in the 1950s for its view, which is today obscured by trees. Garry Johnson had to hike further up the hill to get the photograph above.

THE TOWN AND ITS BEGINNINGS

Much local history is represented at the foot of Morro Bay Boulevard. From the bluff, one sees the rock and the Embarcadero. To the right is Dorn's Restaurant, formerly the Breakers. In the 1920s, it was A. Manford Brown's home and real estate office (see page 65). Down the Centennial Staircase is the giant chessboard. In the 1920s, a restaurant shaped like a ship was built there. It was operated by Basil and Henrietta Jackson (see the back cover.) (Then, courtesy the Dorn family.)

Harry and Dave Leiter opened Morro Bay's first drugstore in the late 1920s. The little store became one of the social centers of town, as everyone shopped there. Dave and his wife operated the store until Joe and Kathryn Limon bought it in 1953. The Limons built this new Rexall drugstore just two blocks down the street in 1963 and stayed in business for 42 years. The building was demolished in 2004 to make way for the Ascot Inn. (Then, courtesy Kathryn Limon; now, courtesy Thom Ream.)

Morro Bay Boulevard has been the center of commerce since William Maston built the first general store (see page 11). The white building on the right with the false front is the Golden Hour Theatre, so named by Noma Stocking. It also served as a movie house and a dance hall. Across the street are Charles Stocking's garage and the Creath brothers' home furnishing store. The current photograph shows the street looking east during the annual car show. (Then, courtesy Juanita Tolle.)

The vintage image looks north along Main Street about 1930. Maston's first store (see page 11) has become Morro Bay Grocery. The young shopkeeper looking into the "Tin Lizzie" is in front of the new Maston's grocery store. The large building to the left of center is Happy Jack's, then the roughest bar in town. In the modern image, the grocery store is now gone. The large white building is actually the next store up Morro Bay Boulevard. (Then, courtesy Juanita Tolle.)

THE TOWN AND ITS BEGINNINGS

In 1929, English immigrant Miles Castle purchased 2.5 acres north of town for $400. There he built an adobe house using the "rammed earth" method rather than the more traditional bricks. This 1945 picture shows Miles, his wife, Jean, and one of the authors of this book, Roger. The house, minus the ivy and surrounded by trees and other houses, is today home to Nancy Castle, Roger's sister. (Then, courtesy Roger Castle.)

In 1946, while visiting in town, Coy and Inez House found and bought this cleaning business. For three weeks they slept on the floor at night and rearranged the shop each morning before opening. For 41 years, Coy House was a familiar sight, pressing shirts in the window, clouds of steam venting out front. The building still exists, essentially unchanged, and is now home to the Sunfire Gallery. (Then, courtesy Inez House; now, courtesy Thom Ream.)

THE TOWN AND ITS BEGINNINGS

Morro Bay's early post offices were often in the corners of various stores. The first was moved and still survives as a private residence on Bella Vista Drive. This *c.* 1900 false-fronted building was at Morro Bay Boulevard and Morro Street, the same location as the 1927 Anderson building (see page 12). In the 1950s, the post office was a modern glass-fronted building at the upper end of that block. The current post office on Napa Street was built in the 1960s. (Then, courtesy Rosemary and Kay Thorn; now, courtesy Thom Ream.)

In 1913, women's suffragist and pioneer developer E. G. Lewis purchased the ranch land that was to become Atascadero. As a way to entice buyers to his Atascadero Colony, Lewis purchased 463 acres of beachfront land just north of Morro Creek in 1919. Although 20 miles west of the Atascadero Colony and over the coast range, E. G. Lewis called this area Atascadero Beach. Pictures of Morro Rock and the beach appeared in his Atascadero brochures without mention of the drive. (Then, courtesy Juanita Tolle.)

THE TOWN AND ITS BEGINNINGS

E. G. Lewis built the Cloisters Inn, a resort hotel and restaurant, several detached beach cottage rooms, and one model home. Part of the land was divided into 40-foot-by-60-foot lots. Paved roads with gutters and streetlights were built, but no other services (not even water) were provided. Only parts of the roads and gutters survive, as does the grove of eucalyptus trees that led to the inn. (Then, courtesy Juanita Tolle.)

There was at least one auction, held in 1927, with lots going for $250 to $300. With other beachfront lots selling for as much as $1,000, the auction generated considerable interest. Some accounts say as many as 400 people showed up. Many lots were sold, but no homes were ever built. Some of Lewis's ideas were finally realized in the 1990s when a modern park and a residential development called the Cloisters was built. (Then, courtesy Juanita Tolle.)

THE TOWN AND ITS BEGINNINGS

Facing legal problems, Lewis lost the development to the state in 1928. Water and sewer services were financed under the Mattoon Act, which subjected all properties to a lien if any one defaulted. With the Depression in 1929, many properties defaulted, and the resulting legal encumbrances were not resolved until the 1950s. The site of the inn is now a public parking lot and beach access area. (Then, courtesy Juanita Tolle.)

According to historian Vic Hanson, the building operated under the name Morro Beach Inn as a grand restaurant and nightclub. During World War II, a regiment of coast artillery was billeted there. The inn, its cottages, and the model home were abandoned after the war. The abandoned inn soon became an enticing source for hard-to-find building materials. There was at least one fire. Now only memories and the suggestion of foundations exist at the end of present-day San Jacinto Street. (Then, courtesy Juanita Tolle.)

THE TOWN AND ITS BEGINNINGS

CHAPTER 2

THE PEOPLE AND WHAT THEY DO

In any small town, it is primarily the people who give it character. In the heady and bustling 1920s, welcoming visitors, especially possible future residents, was everyone's job. Most people had more than one role, everyone knew everyone, and a person's actions affected everyone. This chapter explores what locals and visitors did in early Morro Bay. (Then, courtesy Juanita Tolle.)

At the beginning of the century, the Pismo clam was so abundant that according to historian Lynne Landwehr, riding a buggy "along the sand at low tide felt very much like riding on a cobblestone street." In the 1950s, scenes like the one above were common. The specialized clam fork and a tote bag were a visitor necessity, like today's surfboards and beach chairs. (Then, courtesy Wayne Bickford; now, courtesy Mike Jones.)

THE PEOPLE AND WHAT THEY DO

Until the late 1950s, camping was allowed anywhere on the beach, including what is now Coleman Park and the parking lot at the base of the Rock. Camping is now restricted to a small campground at the extreme north end of town at the state park. Sunbathing, running, surfing, and beachcombing are now the main activities seen on Morro Bay beaches. (Then, courtesy History Center of San Luis Obispo County.)

The subject of the undated photograph below is identified as Annie Schneider Woods, who was the daughter of a prominent early settler. Annie was often seen around town in this buggy. The broad beach just north of Morro Rock was ideal for horses and buggies and later automobiles. (See page 38.) Morro Bay currently has no vehicle accessible beaches but does host an annual kite festival and parade. (Then, courtesy Historical Society of Morro Bay.)

THE PEOPLE AND WHAT THEY DO

Morro Bay has been a visitor destination since the 1880s. Residents of the San Joaquin Valley are particularly fond of the area, enjoying the cool weather and the water. These 1890 vacationers are identified by historian Jane Bailey as the Singleton and McGee families and friends from Tulare. The only real changes shown here are the development on the hillsides and the bathing costumes. (Then, courtesy Historical Society of Morro Bay)

A brisk ride along the beach always has been a popular pastime. Modes of transportation included horseback, horse and buggy (see page 36), or modern motorcar. This picture was one used in advertising real estate opportunities in Morro Bay and is from the collection of William "Bill" Roy. While driving on the beach is no longer allowed, the normally protected and calm bay is ideal for kayaking and other small pleasure craft activities. (Then, courtesy Juanita Tolle.)

THE PEOPLE AND WHAT THEY DO

Morro Bay has always been home to active and artistic people. Even in the hardest of times, people found pleasure and friendship in group activities, like this 1940 city league baseball team. Funded by donations, the team played other such teams from nearby cities. Today the city recreation and parks department sponsors many activities. Church, school, and private groups also provide opportunities for fellowship and self improvement, like this church-sponsored softball team. (Then, courtesy Wayne Bickford; now, courtesy Gary Ream.)

An aging single-family residence served as the fire department offices for many years. The old equipment bay, which had served the city for more than 70 years, was severely damaged in the 2003 San Simeon earthquake. The department used portable buildings and tents for the next five years. Phase one of a two-phase replacement project was completed in 2008. Construction was financed by a FEMA grant and a combination of city monies, department fund-raising, and private donations.

Fire department personnel burn down their damaged old quarters in 2007 after four years of planning and fund-raising for the new complex. They used the opportunity to practice a number of firefighting techniques. The rendering by the architectural firm of Fraser Seiple shows the new administration and crew quarters adjacent to the completed equipment bay. This building will be financed primarily by a $1.6-million federal stimulus grant. (Then, courtesy Morro Bay Fire Department.)

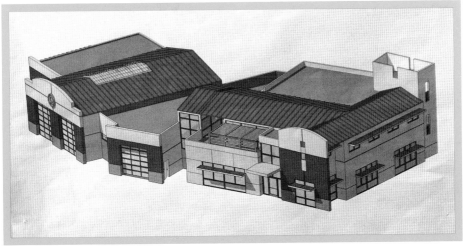

Small towns love parades, and Morro Bay is no exception. The early 1940s picture shows a recently purchased 1939 fire engine. Note the Cracker Box café behind the truck. It was very popular but only had seating for seven. In the new picture the house with the awning still exists, but two new buildings have replaced the restaurant. (Then, courtesy Juanita Tolle.)

Morro Bay did have a small airport for a few years. It was located on the Domenghini ranch at the southern entrance to town on what is now Highway 1. It was a project the eldest son, Louis, created about 1940 to foster his interest in flying. It also served the occasional private aircraft and as a base for crop-dusting planes until the freeway was built in the late 1950s. (See page 19.) (Then, courtesy Betty Domenghini.)

Basically only two things have changed about the business of underwater fishing—the size and variety of the catch and the equipment. In the 1930s, Glenn Bickford put on a heavy suit with a sealed hard hat to collect abalone. His air supply came through a hose from the boat above. Today Jeremiah O'Brien wears a skintight suit festooned with equipment to collect sea urchins and other delicacies. He carries his air supply with him. (Then, courtesy Karen Perlette; now, courtesy Jeremiah O'Brien.)

THE PEOPLE AND WHAT THEY DO

From the 1930s to about 1955, the abalone industry was big business. Commercial abalone diving was done from small boats. Pictured around 1957 is the *Nina*, one of Barney Clancy's "black fleet" operating out of Morro Bay. A three-man crew consisting of a diver, the diver's tender, and the boat operator were standard practice. Today the abalone population had declined greatly and underwater fishing is a one-man operation. (Then, courtesy Steve Rebuck; now, courtesy Jeremiah O'Brien.)

Commercial abalone harvesting and processing was a major industry in Morro Bay. Published studies show that Morro Bay red abalone landings averaged 2 million pounds a year for more than 50 years. In this 1950s photograph, Charlie Pierce unloads processed shells. The reasons for the population decline in the mid-1950s are many and complex, and agreement on cause, effect, and cure is still elusive today. Today's harvests, like this shown by Trudi O'Brien, are smaller and harder to find. (Then, courtesy Steve Rebuck; now, courtesy Jeremiah O'Brien.)

THE PEOPLE AND WHAT THEY DO

Although they carry new and sophisticated equipment, the basic tool of the fishing industry, the boats, have changed little. In this old picture, the *New Roma*, with a purse seine net, hoists the day's catch. Today the trawler *Diane Susan* looks much the same as line fishing boats from the 1940s and 1950s. (Then, courtesy History Center of San Luis Obispo County.)

Early underwater harvesting was hard work. The hard-hat diver of old put his catch into a small net. Then, wearing 150 pounds of equipment and weights, he would return to the boat above. With help from his tender, he would bring the net up the short iron steps and into the boat. A diver's gear today is more sophisticated and much lighter (see page 44). In the picture above, a large harvest of sea urchins was hauled aboard with the help of a mechanical hoist. (Then, courtesy Wayne Bickford; now, courtesy Jeremiah O'Brien.)

THE PEOPLE AND WHAT THEY DO

The Nagano brothers were the first to grow artichokes in Morro Bay. They grew well in the flat land bordering Morro Creek. The rich soil and the flat land along Morro Creek were ideal for the popular delicacy. The temperate climate provided a long growing season. That's George, in the center, with his brother Take Eto on the left and an unidentified friend on the right. The land is still in use today not only for artichokes but for flower seed, feed crops, peas, beans, and sugar beets. (Then, courtesy Pat Nagano.)

This is the northern breakwater in 1951. Storms in 1955 and 1956 caused significant damage and more stone was taken from the Rock for repairs. Fishermen, like Joseph Gerber seen here, and sightseers are now discouraged from venturing into the area. Even on calm days like this, occasional waves breech the barrier. (Then, courtesy John Gerber.)

Storm-driven ocean waves are one of nature's most powerful and relentless forces. This photograph was taken after a particularly strong storm in 1954. The power of these waves had displaced tons of rock off the breakwater. Note how a whole section of rock at the tip of the breakwater has been moved eastward several feet. That storm washed over the naturally protective sand spit. The sand spit and breakwater eventually got extensive repairs and still protect the harbor today. (Then, courtesy Juanita Tolle; now, courtesy Thom Ream.)

In 1875, Franklin Riley planted several eucalyptus trees around the town, including a double row down Morro Bay Boulevard. This tree at Kern Avenue and Morro Bay Boulevard was the last survivor of those rows. Several large groves of theses trees were planted on the central California coast. The growers hoped to harvest ship masts from the tall trees, but the wood proved unsuitable. (Both, courtesy Thom Ream.)

EUCALYPTUS GLOBULUS
SEED FROM AUSTRALIA
SURVIVOR OF A DOUBLE ROW
PLANTED ABOUT 1875
BY
FRANKLIN RILEY

The city placed a plaque at the base of the tree. In 2001, it was discovered that fungus had infected its root system, and it was taken down in 2002. All that remains is a stump. When the tree was removed, five large sections of the massive 125-year-old trunk were shaped into benches. They can be seen and used in various parts of town, as Gary Ream is doing here. (Then, courtesy Thom Ream.)

The first Morro Bay-San Luis Obispo highway was completed in 1923. This photograph was taken near the north entrance to Cuesta Community College. A trip to the county seat and back took most of a day until well into the 1950s, although part of the road was widened to four lanes during World War II. The remainder of the freeway to Morro Bay was completed about 1960. The new road is now about 100 yards east of the old. (Then, courtesy Juanita Tolle.)

Yoshio (George) Nagano and his wife, Kanaru, came to California from Japan in 1913, and they farmed northeast of town. His second son, Pat, is shown below with his aunt. Pat enlisted in the army in 1941 and served as a translator. Most of his family was forced by the government to relocate to an internment camp, but the farm was cared for by neighbors. After the war, Pat resumed farming and served many years on the local school board. (Then, courtesy Pat Nagano.)

After the attack on Pearl Harbor, the town held this parade in support of the local military base. In 1940, the navy established an amphibious training base on 100 acres of waterfront land. By the end of the war, it would occupy more than 250 acres and provide many improvements to the town. More than 60 years later, the town still loves parades, such as this seventh annual Celebrate Morro Bay parade originated by the historical society. (Then, courtesy Historical Society of Morro Bay.)

Another important enterprise from the beginning of Morro Bay was ranching. The low rolling hills and mild climate were ideal for cattle and feed. Cattle ranching has changed little over the years. Remnants of old wooden fences and barbed wire are in use everywhere and are only supplemented with steel gates. This roundup at the San Luisito Ranch in 2009 still has many of the elements of the one at Domenghini ranch in 1969. (Then, courtesy Betty Domenghini.)

A point of city pride is the championship golf course. In 1928, Edward Murphy and Clinton Miller, developers of the Heights, opened the first nine holes and elegant clubhouse on White's Point. William "Bill" Roy was a major player in the conception and construction of the course. Bill had worked for Miller and Murphy and T. J. Lawrence. He was also the force behind the navy base being built in Morro Bay. Bill is pictured putting on the ninth hole. (Then, courtesy Juanita Tolle.)

THE PEOPLE AND WHAT THEY DO

The course was created on the southwest-facing slope of Back Hill on land T. J. Lawrence had once planned for homes. The first nine holes cost $140,000 and the clubhouse another $10,000. The course was enlarged to a full 18 holes in 1951 and a new clubhouse built up on the hill. Parts of the old clubhouse were moved onto the state park as employee residences. (Then, courtesy Juanita Tolle.)

Political and financial maneuvering for a state park in Morro Bay began in 1928 when state voters approved a bond issue to buy such lands. The present park land was finally purchased in 1934 from the bankrupt Miller and Murphy real estate company. Campsites and stone restrooms were constructed by the Works Progress Administration and the California Conservation Corps, and the park was completed about 1936.

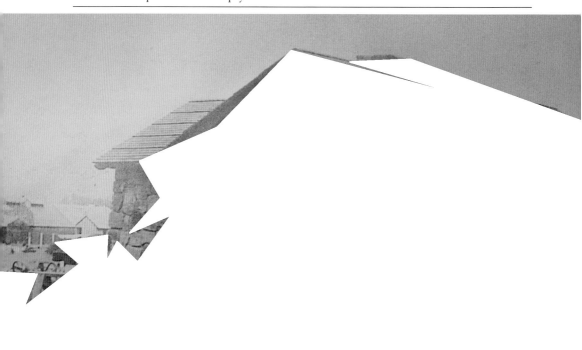

THE PEOPLE AND WHAT THEY DO

Russell Noyes was the first chief ranger of the new Morro Bay State Park. His wife was a well-known real estate agent. In addition to his duties as chief ranger, Russell was also one of the managers of the golf course. He and his wife lived for a time in the original clubhouse, located near where the Morro Bay State Park Museum of Natural History is today. The current park manager, Rouvaishyana, is shown here on the museum walkway. (Then, courtesy History Center of San Luis Obispo County.)

An elected constable policed Morro Bay in the early years. Several early pioneers served in this post. The first may have been H. Y. Stanley, followed by Franklin Riley. The vintage image shows Danish immigrant Ivar Holt, who was elected in 1926. The county sheriff's department filled the role until 1964. The current city police force consists of 18 officers plus support staff. Pictured here in front of the station remodeled in 2003 are Sgt. Bryan Millard and officer Stephanie Pipan. (Then, photograph by Janice Cooper; courtesy Adele Sylva Costa.)

CHAPTER 3

THE ROCK AND THE HARBOR

The Embarcadero, the bay-side business district, is a legacy of the war years. The navy established a training base, expanded the existing land and road, and built the two "T" piers. In this 1976 picture, the small tower holds equipment for landing the day's catch. The large building to the right is the Great American Fish Company restaurant. (Then, courtesy Wayne Bickford.)

Bring together the open waters of Morro Bay, a stiff wind or a powerful motor, and a sunny day, and the race is on. Residents and visitors alike have enjoyed the competition from this late 1940s power boat race to the more elegant sailboat races of today. Note the pier-like structure on the sand spit, left of the rock. That was the last remnant of a pedestrian walkway across the bay built by the navy in 1942. (Then, courtesy Bud and Lynne Laster.)

This view of the rock is from the west end of Morro Bay Boulevard. In 1925, this was the home and office of Kate and A. Manford Brown, who was a prominent realtor. Later it would be the site of the original Breakers Café, now Dorn's. Historian Vic Hanson attributes the original photograph to Lillie Brown Anderson (see page 21). (Then, courtesy Juanita Tolle.)

Excursions to the sand spit and around the bay have always been popular. This water taxi, with an unusual rear paddle wheel for propulsion, was likely financed by 1920s real estate interests as a means of showing the bay to prospective buyers. The floating restaurant, the *Chablis*, provides similar services today. (Then, courtesy Juanita Tolle.)

The Rock and the Harbor

Several water taxis were available in the 1920s to take visitors on a tour around the bay or over to the sand spit for a picnic. This one was owned and operated by three expatriate Englishmen, Tommy Thomas, Basil Jackson, and Sydney Nichols. Note how the bay extends right up to the bluff on the town side. The modern craft is the *Papagallo II*, owned by Leonard and Midge Geniteu. (Then, courtesy Juanita Tolle.)

This photograph marked "Morro Bay Fish Market 1925" was likely taken at the foot of Harbor Street. In the early days of the town, there were three or four piers along the narrow bay-side road that would become the Embarcadero. The first, according to historian D. L. Gates, was the pier belonging to Franklin Williams and Captain Riley at the foot of Morro Bay Boulevard. Al Sylva's pier was just south of the foot of present-day Beach Street in the area shown above. (Then, courtesy Juanita Tolle.)

THE ROCK AND THE HARBOR

These pictures clearly show how the land was filled in below the bluff to provide access to the bay. The water here is shallow and mud flats appear at low tide. The new picture was taken from the bluff at the end of Olive Street. This is near the Tidelands City Park at the south end of the Embarcadero. This park supports pleasure craft and sport fishing and has facilities for launching small boats. (Then, courtesy Historical Society of Morro Bay.)

In 1940, the navy began construction of a training base here. Following World War II, the county sold the land to the Pacific Gas and Electric Company for $44 million. In 1953, as seen here, construction was begun on an electricity generating plant cooled by water from the bay. Today the plant with its three smoke stacks has become a second symbol of Morro Bay. It remains a blessing and a curse, providing tax revenue but occupying prime waterfront land. (Then, courtesy Juanita Tolle.)

On the morning of December 1, 1988, fire consumed the south "T" pier. One man died, and several people were injured. The fast-burning fire destroyed or damaged 13 boats. Nine were saved by the efforts of many area firefighters and responding fishermen. Fate put fire engineer Mike Pond in charge that morning. Under his leadership, the fire was confined to the area and the Great American Fish Company restaurant was saved. Mike Pond is currently the Morro Bay fire chief. (Then, courtesy the *Sun Bulletin*.)

The first major construction operation in the bay began in 1890, when rock was needed for breakwaters at Port Hartford (now Avila Beach). The tugboat *Liberty* is seen on the facing page. The mast-like derrick was used to load the blasted rock onto another barge for the trip south to Avila.

The only industrial operation in the bay today is periodic dredging to keep the channels open. Equipment from the 2010 project is shown in the current picture. (Then, courtesy Historical Society of Morro Bay; now, courtesy Thom Ream.)

Between 1890 and 1936 more than 1 million tons of rock was taken for various projects. Quarrying was officially banned in 1963. As early as 1910, due to an accident, it was discovered that blocking the north channel improved harbor conditions. In 1936, a WPA project used rubble from years of quarrying to create a narrow, rocky causeway (see page 50). This remained through the war years and was expanded with dredging tailings in the 1950s. (Then, courtesy Historical Society of Morro Bay; now, courtesy Thom Ream.)

Morro Rock is one of the most iconic and photographed natural features in the world. It is the town's permanent and nearly unchanging logo. While the rock in these pictures, taken 100 years apart, may appear identical, old-timers can easily see the effects of 40 years of quarrying.

Compare the area just below the large dark patch of vegetation; changes to the shoreline are easier to see. The man-made Embarcadero is today home to a wide variety of tourist and fishing-related businesses. (Then, courtesy Historical Society of Morro Bay.)

THE ROCK AND THE HARBOR

The Embarcadero, Morro Bay's harbor and commercial area, was a legacy from the navy presence here. The parking lot seen here, now Giovanni's Fish Market, was tidal land when the town was first established. The navy completed the creation of most of the Embarcadero and the causeway out to Morro Rock. The town piers were also constructed by the navy (see pages 78 and 79). (Then, courtesy Historical Society of Morro Bay; now, courtesy Thom Ream.)

The growth of the fishing fleet after World War II was explosive. By 1950, more than 150 boats called Morro Bay their home port. Multiple docks along the water's edge supplemented moorings on the south "T" pier. Today a half-dozen trawlers and one sailboat are visible from the same angle.

The commercial fishing industry has always been subject to political and natural cycles. Development of tourism has helped stabilize Morro Bay's economy. Note the undeveloped bluff by Beach Street. (Then, courtesy Juanita Tolle.)

This early photograph was taken from Eagle Rock, the rocky rise just off south Main Street. Note the open channel north of the rock. The Joseph C. Stocking ranch is seen by the bluff. The large building in the upper right is his grain warehouse. Just visible is the wooden slip used to slide grain sacks down the bluff into the schooner's holds. Residences and trees have changed the view from Eagle Rock today. (Then, courtesy Historical Society of Morro Bay.)

One of the most enduring legacies of the navy base was the construction of the "T" piers. The piers were wide and open to accommodate large numbers of trainees. They would assemble on what is now the harbor parking lot and then move out onto the pier for training. Note the headquarters buildings up on the bluff. Today the wide dock serves well for mooring and fishing. (Then, courtesy Historical Society of Morro Bay.)

THE ROCK AND THE HARBOR

Originally one T-shaped and one L-shaped pier were built to train troops in embarkation and debarkation techniques. The south pier had a two-story scaffolding with a sheer wall on the bay side to simulate the side of a troop transport ship. Trainees would assemble on this dock and practice debarkation using rope nets. Troops were brought up from the beach in small boats to practice embarkation. (Then, courtesy Historical Society of Morro Bay.)

Years of weather and sea action built up large sand dunes on the wide beach north of the rock—some larger than the ones in this 1920s picture. Some of the wind-built dunes were as much as 30 feet high. It was a favorite play area for those who lived and grew up here during the 1950s. Natural forces, development, and construction of the power plant all led to the decline of this natural resource. (Then, courtesy Juanita Tolle.)

4

THE BAY AND
THE BACK BAY

Morro Bay is the only naturally protected harbor between San Francisco and Mission Bay near San Diego. Its calm waters are relatively shallow, the main channel averaging only 20 to 40 feet. It is 4 miles long and covers 10 square miles with many idyllic vistas. This 1920s view of Capt. Clark Church's wharf at the foot of Harbor Street is typical. (Then, courtesy Juanita Tolle.)

This aerial view of Morro Rock was taken by Wayne Bickford about 1956. Note the heavy storm damage to the breakwater and the sand spit. The original breakwater had been made with granite from Morro Rock around 1900. Later repairs were made with softer and lighter basalt. The strong storms of 1955–1956 pushed much of that material into the bay, allowing waves to break through the sand spit. Subsequent repairs were better engineered and endure to today. (Then, courtesy Juanita Tolle; now, courtesy Forrest L. Doud.)

THE BAY AND THE BACK BAY

At high or moderate tides, it has always been possible to get shallow-draft craft like kayaks or canoes south across the bay to Los Osos (see page 85). However, lack of landing facilities (not to mention commercial motivation) makes this a rare occurrence. The southeast section is part of the Chorro Creek estuary, partially shown in the modern image. The tree-studded area is the state park, and the golf course is to the right. (Then, courtesy Juanita Tolle; now, courtesy Lynda Roeller.)

THE BAY AND THE BACK BAY

Here is another dramatic view of the damage following the 1955–1956 storms. Note that work on phase two of the PG&E plant had not begun. The land immediately north of the plant shows no development (see page 31). Repairs to the breakwater were not completed until the 1960s. In the picture above, the development of the Atascadero Beach parcel is evident. The rectangle bounded by trees is the high school. (Then, courtesy Juanita Tolle; now, courtesy Lynda Roeller.)

In the early 1920s, just as Morro Bay was being developed, Richard Otto bought his first lot in the future Baywood Park from Walter Redfield. By the mid-1920s, Otto owned 1,000 acres along the bay and had graded it into lots. Redfield's remaining property became the village of Los Osos further inland. Always bedroom communities of San Luis Obispo, an explosion of development in the 1970s and 1980s effectively merged the two communities, but a friendly rivalry still exists. (Then, courtesy Juanita Tolle; now, courtesy Lynda Roeller.)

In the *c.* 1920 picture, note the open north channel by the rock. The Embarcadero is not built, and the main channel is along the shoreline, partly obscured by trees. There is limited development on the Heights above the little town amongst the trees. In the foreground is the land that would become the state park and golf course. In the modern photograph, the rocky area to the right is Black Hill with the golf course to the left. (Then, courtesy Juanita Tolle; now, courtesy Lynda Roeller.)

THE BAY AND THE BACK BAY

Alfred Sylva (or Silva) leased an older pier at the foot of Morro Bay Boulevard in the early 1900s. In this view most of the lands are tidal mud flats. Only a narrow road runs in front of the net sheds. It was so narrow that there was no place to turn a truck around. In the modern picture, the public restrooms stand about where the shed was. (Then, courtesy Historical Society of Morro Bay.)

In 1949, real estate salesman, golf and country club manager, and expatriate Scotsman William "Bill" Roy worked to get permission from the state park to build a marina south of White's Point. This postcard view from the early 1950s shows the result. Today the marina is still a popular and convenient dock for pleasure craft of all kinds. The 1950s-era house is now the popular Bayside Café. (Then, courtesy Historical Society of Morro Bay.)

This is a more modern view of the marina, from perhaps the late 1980s. The land in the background is the Morro Bay National Estuary. Fed by the Chorro and Los Osos Valley Creeks, it is the third largest national estuary in the nation. Morro Bay is designated as a bird sanctuary, and the estuary is home to more than 250 species of birds. (Then, courtesy Historical Society of Morro Bay.)

One of the unspoiled—indeed practically unchanged—bits of shoreline on the bay is this area north of the Morro Bay State Park Museum of Natural History. The tree-covered rocky hill to the left is Eagle Rock. From the early days of the town, the land behind the trees was the Mathias Schneider ranch. Later Robert Fairbanks bought a portion and built a fine craftsman-style home. The rest of the beachfront

became part of the state park in 1934. Today the area is popular with bird watchers, kayakers, and other sightseers. Part of Schneider's land became the Inn at Morro Bay. The Fairbanks property was taken into the state park and became a protected heron rookery. The Fairbanks house was razed in the 1970s to protect the rookery. (Then, courtesy Juanita Tolle.)

THE BAY AND THE BACK BAY

The Morro Bay State Park Museum of Natural History on White's Point was opened in 1960. This low tide view of it from the bay has changed little over the years. Oysters occurred naturally in these mud flats, and there is historical evidence that they were a favorite food of the native Chumash Indians. As natural numbers of the delicacy began to dwindle in the 1930s, likely due to environmental causes, the mud flats of the back bay were used for commercial oyster farming. (Then, courtesy Jean Connelly.)

THE BAY AND THE BACK BAY

The most prominent local oyster farmers were the Leage family. From 1953 until they sold the business in 2001, they grew Pacific oysters in these mud flats. They raised the mollusk from seed (called "spat") imported mainly from Washington state. In those days, mature oysters were harvested by hand. Today oysters are grown in large net sacks laid out in rows, which makes harvesting more efficient. (Then, courtesy Jean Connelly.)

Franklin Riley founded the town because he had a vision of the future. This has been true of each generation of the town's leaders. The real estate interests of the 1920s reflected the popular ideas of their times, and several attempts were made to exploit the commercial potentials of the natural harbor. Each time, money, politics, and/or national events would derail those plans. Eventually popular trends and leadership converged, and Morro Bay became the quiet hometown and tourist destination it was meant to be. (Then, courtesy Juanita Tolle; now, courtesy Lynda Roeller.)

THE BAY AND THE BACK BAY

Those of us who call Morro Bay home, whether natives or immigrants, are thankful that we do not live here, in the Morro Bay that never was. (Courtesy Schani Siong.)

www.arcadiapublishing.com

Discover books about the town where you grew up, the cities where your friends and families live, the town where your parents met, or even that retirement spot you've been dreaming about. Our Web site provides history lovers with exclusive deals, advanced notification about new titles, e-mail alerts of author events, and much more.

Find Your Place in History.